I0201036

THE PRAYING ATHLETE
QUOTE BOOK

VOL 4

KEEPING THE RIGHT
MENTALITY

Copyright © 2019 by Robert B. Walker

All rights reserved. No part of this publication may be reproduced, stored in a retrieval system, or transmitted in any form or by any means — electronic, mechanical, photocopy, recording, or any other — except for brief quotation in printed reviews, without the prior written permission of the publisher.

Unless otherwise indicated, Scripture quotations in this book are taken from The Holy Bible, *New International Version®, NIV®*. Copyright © 1973, 1978, 1984, 2011 by Biblica, Inc.™ Used by permission. All rights reserved worldwide.

Published by The Core Media Group, Inc., P.O. Box 2037, Indian Trail, NC 28079.

Cover & Interior Design: Ashlyn Helms

Printed in the United States of America.

VOL 4 KEEPING THE RIGHT MENTALITY

Be confident, for today did not come by chance, but rather through the time and commitment to walk this journey of hard work and dedication to perfect the talents God gave you.

People don't know what it costs to be you. They don't know the sacrifices you made along the way. All they see is the smile on your face, because being you is cool when you know what it costs.

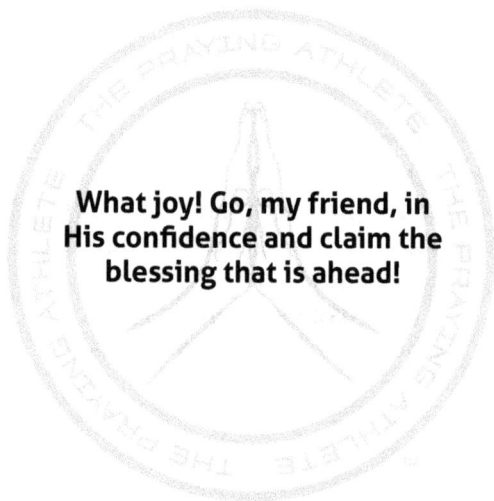

What joy! Go, my friend, in His confidence and claim the blessing that is ahead!

Respond believing you can and you will, knowing nothing can make you respond in a negative way because you have dreams and goals to achieve.

Regret is a tough thing to live with. If you live life not wanting to live with regret, you will find yourself taking chances and living life to the fullest.

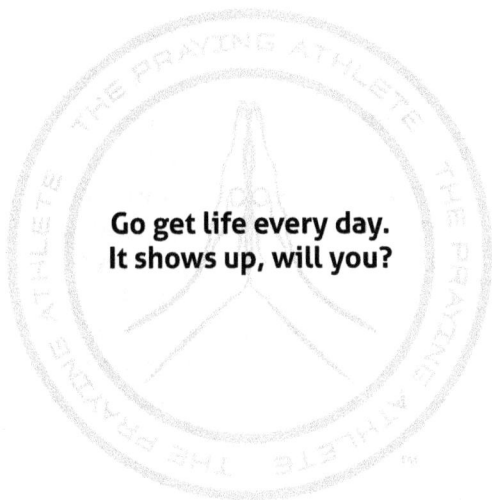

**Go get life every day.
It shows up, will you?**

The blessings of life ahead will allow you to impact people for me. Be confident in the tests I have ahead for you, embrace the rushing waters of life as I rush my goodness into your life. May you hear my voice as you hear the waters and may my spirit move and consume your life.

Always work on your
negotiating skills. I get
something free wherever I go.
Just last night the restaurant
was closing. I asked if there
were any care packages as I
go. She said no. I said, surely
there is something.
She said yes, okay, and she
brought me a big box of fresh
baked cookies that had not
been sold that day.
Asking is a key ingredient to
some of the best
things you ever taste.

When you give up, you may
feel like life ripped you off.
However, it is time to step up
and step back into life.

I am going somewhere
because the Word says I am.

**You want to be better,
but at what price?**

I may not be happy today, but I am content because I know and believe many good days are ahead, no matter what this day may hold.

We all want express success, but no success comes without pressing.

Every day, rise with
anticipation for the day
you have been granted.
Just breathe and feel the
air in your lungs.

**Has adversity
discouraged you?
If so, say
"This will not conquer me.
This I shall overcome."**

It is the things that are
invisible that we worry about
99 percent of the time -
the unknown.
Live in the present, and you
will be confident 99 percent
of the time.

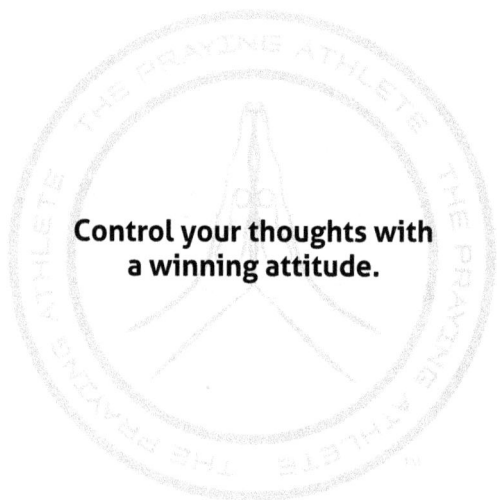

**Control your thoughts with
a winning attitude.**

Embrace everything that happens, but do not consume everything that happens.

Prepare with the process in mind, but know the process before you prepare.

Confront obstacles head on so that you can see clearly.

**Imagine where you want
to go, then go.**

**Do you want it?
Then EARN it with maximum
effort during every waking
moment of your life.
Why not?
You said you want it, right?
This is how you earn it!**

What makes a successful business person? It is simple: do things that others think are below them or mundane. The business person can see the need to do the task in order for others to be successful.

Take Charge! Live life focused
on your lifetime, not the
minutes and moments of life.
If you make choices through
the lens of your lifetime, and
not the lens of the moment, it
will enable you to take charge
of your life and protect
your heart from the painful
choices you make in a
moment of weakness.
Find your strength by
taking charge and
guarding your heart.

**The seemingly insignificant
choices you make every day
are determining whether
or not you are fulfilling
your destiny.**

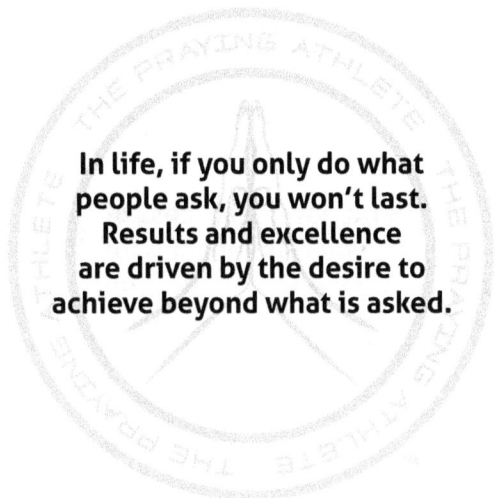

In life, if you only do what
people ask, you won't last.
Results and excellence
are driven by the desire to
achieve beyond what is asked.

**Pray for the success of
those you can impact with the
success God grants you.**

**Ask your loved ones how
you can show your
love for them.**

We all start to
complain when we compare
ourselves to others.
Stop comparing and start
sharing all the goodness you
have to give away.

Yesterday is now gone,
embrace this new day with an
incredible sense of urgency
to overcome any barriers that
made yesterday or any day,
a challenge.

THOUGHTS & REFLECTIONS

_____

_____

_____

_____

_____

_____

_____

_____

_____

_____

_____

_____

_____

_____

_____

_____

_____

_____

_____

_____

_____

_____

_____

_____

_____

_____

_____

_____

_____

_____

_____

_____

_____

_____

_____

_____

_____

_____

_____

_____

_____

_____

_____

_____

_____

_____

_____

_____

_____

_____

_____

_____

_____

MY QUOTES

_____

_____

_____

_____

_____

_____

_____

_____

_____

_____

_____

_____

_____

_____

_____

_____

_____

_____

_____

_____

_____

_____

_____

_____

_____

_____

_____

_____

_____

_____

_____

_____

ACKNOWLEDGEMENTS

I want to acknowledge and say thank you to all those that helped with this project:

Nadia Guy
Ashlyn Helms
My Mom & Dad

All of my NFL Clients, current and former, that have encouraged me to share these words with others.

ABOUT
TPA

The Praying Athlete is a movement that creates an organic culture of prayer through an uplifting community and authentic conversation.

For more information, visit our website **www.theprayingathlete.com**.

Follow us on social media.

@ThePrayingAthlete

@Praying_Athlete

@ThePrayingAthlete

COLLECT ALL

8 VOL.

Our first volume of *The Praying Athlete Quote Book* addresses the topic of playing the game. Quotes and thoughts from Robert B. Walker, paired with Scripture from God's Word, allow readers to get a good idea about what playing a good game looks like.

Our second volume of *The Praying Athlete Quote Book* addresses the topic of teamwork. Quotes and thoughts from Robert B. Walker, paired with Scripture from God's Word, allow readers to understand what it means to be a good teammate and surround yourself with people who lift you up.

Our third volume of *The Praying Athlete Quote Book* addresses the topic of growth & preparation for the future. Quotes and thoughts from Robert B. Walker, paired with Scripture from God's Word, allow readers to know that even though the future is uncertain, there is a plan and purpose for everyone.

Our fourth volume of *The Praying Athlete Quote Book* addresses the topic of keeping the right mentality. Quotes and thoughts from Robert B. Walker allow readers to understand how staying in the right mindset can improve overall performance.

Our fifth volume of *The Praying Athlete Quote Book* addresses the topic of staying motivated. Quotes and thoughts from Robert B. Walker allow readers to become motivated to accomplish their goals, even when they feel they are not up to the task.

Our sixth volume of *The Praying Athlete Quote Book* addresses the topic of personal accountability. Quotes and thoughts from Robert B. Walker allow readers to think about how they can better themselves. Whether its ending a bad habit or saying no to anything that may hurt themselves or others, staying accountable will benefit one's character and performance.

Our seventh volume of *The Praying Athlete Quote Book* addresses the topic of living life. This volume is the first part in a two part living life series. Quotes and thoughts from Robert B. Walker give readers a better understanding of how to live life to the fullest.

Our eighth volume of *The Praying Athlete Quote Book* addresses the topic of living life. This volume is the second part in a two part living life series. Quotes and thoughts from Robert B. Walker give readers a better understanding of how to live life to the fullest.

FOR MORE INFO AND MERCHANDISE, PLEASE VISIT
WWW.THEPRAYINGATHLETE.COM

CHECK OUT OUR

THE PRAYING ATHLETE™
PHOTOGRAPHY
QUOTE BOOKS

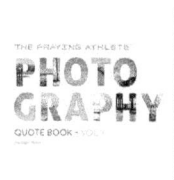

VOL. 1

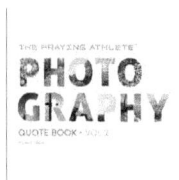

VOL. 2

VOL. 3

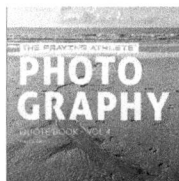

VOL. 4

*The Praying Athlete Photography Quote Book*s celebrate God's glory and magnificence through His creation. They contain photos taken by Robert B. Walker, paired with his words of wisdom, motivation, and inspiration.

FOR MORE INFO AND MERCHANDISE, PLEASE VISIT
WWW.THEPRAYINGATHLETE.COM

www.ingramcontent.com/pod-product-compliance
Lightning Source LLC
Chambersburg PA
CBHW060042040426
42331CB00032B/2195